Wedding Cakes With Lorelie
Step by Step
...

Lorelie Carvey

Cover photo image and photo of Lorelie by John Munno, johnmunnoweddings.com/
Photo of Lorelie in logo by Mike Meken, mekenstudios.com
Logo by Gini Frank Fischer, ginifischer.com
Step-by-step photos by Scott Carvey
Copyright © 2017 Lorelie Carvey

All rights reserved. No part of this publication may be reproduced, stored in a retrieval system, or transmitted by any means—electronic, mechanical, photographic (photocopying), recording, or otherwise—without prior permission in writing from the author.

ISBN: 1540462471
ISBN 13: 9781540462473
Library of Congress Control Number: 2016919631
CreateSpace Independent Publishing Platform
North Charleston, South Carolina

Your book has proved priceless, and all your recipes are spot on. Thank you so much. Probably the best investment anyone interested in cake baking could make.

—Liz Davis

It's a very well-written, clear book, and I love the illustrations, which really help. I'm looking forward to trying all the recipes. Thanks so much.

—Salma

Incredible book. I love it. Your book helped me so much, and you answered all my questions. Incredible. Thank you.

—Leslie De Leon

Your recipes are the best, and my customers are now raving about my cakes. You are a stunning person sharing and helping so much.

—Marlene Cunliff (South Africa)

Thank you so much for your dedication in making the step-by-step explanations. I am a Venezuelan, living in Chile. My husband is Chilean, and we met in France. We share a lovely story topped with the adventure of making our own wedding cake. He helped me all the way through! Thank you for making this experience possible!

—Vanessa (Chile)

Thank you, thank you, thank you. You are my wedding-cake angel.

—Loryn

Many, many thanks for being a helpful voice out there in my scary cake-building moments.

—Joelle

I would definitely recommend your books. They're brilliant. Thanks again, and keep up the great work. Best wishes.

—Sue (England)

Contents

Introduction ix
    Tools x
    Specialty Products and Supplies xii
    Cake-Decorating Supplies xii
    Paper Products xiii
    Baking and Cake-Decorating Terms xiv
    Illustration of Tiers and Layers xvii

Baking Your Cakes 1
    About Ovens 1
    Preparing Your Pans 2
    Making Your Batter 2
    Removing Your Cakes from the Pans 8
Putting Your Cakes Together 11
    Filling and Crumb Coating 11
    Frosting Your Cakes 13
    The Internal Structure of a Wedding Cake 16
Stacking Your Cakes 17
    Using Dowels 17
    Decorating Your Cakes 19
    Using Cake Stackers 20
    Delivering Your Cakes 21

Lorelie's Best Recipes 23
Vanilla Cake 27
    Batter Amounts and Multiplying the Vanilla-Cake Recipe ... 29
    Ideas and suggestions for the vanilla-cake recipe 30
Chocolate-Stout Cake 32
    Batter Amounts and Multiplying the Chocolate-Stout Recipe ... 33

Ideas and suggestions for the stout-cake recipe · 35
More ideas · 35
Chocolate-Buttermilk Cake · 36
 Batter Amounts and Multiplying the Chocolate-Buttermilk Recipe · · · · · · · · · · · · 38
 Ideas and suggestions for the chocolate-cake recipe · 39
Carrot Cake · 41
 Batter Amounts and Multiplying the Carrot-Cake Recipe · · · · · · · · · · · · · · · · · · 43
 Ideas and suggestions for the carrot-cake recipe · 44
Hazelnut Cake · 46
 Batter Amounts and Multiplying the Hazelnut-Cake Recipe · · · · · · · · · · · · · · · · 48
 Ideas and suggestions for the hazelnut-cake recipe · 50
Simple Pure-White Cake · 51
 Batter Amounts and Multiplying the Simple White-Cake Recipe · · · · · · · · · · · · · 52
 Ideas and suggestions for the pure-white-cake recipe · 53
Coconut Cake · 54
 Batter Amounts and Multiplying the Coconut-Cake Recipe · · · · · · · · · · · · · · · · 56
 Ideas and suggestions for the coconut-cake recipe · 57
Chocolate Ganache · 59
 Chocolate Ganache for a Wedding Cake · 60
Chocolate Mousse · 61
 Chocolate Mousse for a Wedding Cake · 62
Lemon Cream Cheese · 64
 Lemon Cream-Cheese Filling for a Wedding Cake · 64
Italian Meringue Buttercream · 66
 English Lemon Curd for Flavoring Buttercream · 67
White-Chocolate Buttercream with Fresh Raspberries · 69
 Raspberry Buttercream · 69
Chocolate Buttercream · 71

Afterword · 73
About the Author · 75

Introduction

• • •

THIS HOW-TO BOOK IS WRITTEN with the novice baker and cake decorator in mind but will be a helpful refresher for intermediate and advanced cake decorators as well.

I learned to make wedding cakes at a fancy French pastry shop when I worked there as an assistant cake decorator, and then I baked and decorated from my home kitchen for many years, followed by managing the desserts and wedding cakes at various banquet halls. Preparing, baking, and decorating wedding cakes is one of my greatest passions, and I would love to share it with you.

Keeping it simple is one of the main goals of this book. There is nothing mysterious about constructing a wedding cake, yet it appears to be almost magical. By breaking down the steps for you to follow with helpful tips along the way, I have tried to ensure that baking a wedding cake will not seem so overwhelming.

If you can bake a cake and do simple piping, you can make a wedding cake. With a few little tricks of the trade that I will share with you here, you will be able to create beautiful and delicious cakes like the professionals.

Included in this book are a list of tools and supplies you will need to get started and my most requested and popular wedding-cake recipes with measurements in cups, grams, and ounces.

Your questions about freezing, storing, filling, frosting, decorating, and delivering your wedding-cake creations will be answered in this book. Let's get started.

Tools

Here are the tools and products you will need. These are straight from my inventory list and will be helpful as you get more involved in this craft. You may order through the website at http://www.wedding-cakes-for-you.com/weddingcakesupplies.html.

You will not need all of these right away; you may already have some of the tools in your kitchen. Start with the basics. I've marked them with an *.

- **Cake Racks**—Also called cooling racks, they are made of wire and have short feet that lift them off the counter. When your cakes come out of the oven, you turn them out onto racks to cool. The space under the cooling racks allows air to circulate around the cakes and prevents condensation.
- **Cake Tester**—A thin metal tool used to see if your cakes are done by sticking it into the center of the cakes. If crumbs are attached when you pull it out, your cake is not quite done.
- ***Cake-Cutting Knife**—A long serrated knife for splitting cake layers. Choose a good-quality knife. Ideally you want one that is longer than the diameter of the cake you are cutting.
- **Cake-Decorating Comb**—A flat stainless-steel tool with three sets of serrated edges, used for making decorations in cake frosting.
- ***Candy Thermometer**—A gauge used for measuring the temperature of cooked sugar. Get a high-quality, heavy-duty one. You will need this often for making Italian meringue buttercream.
- **Double Boiler**—A pot that holds hot water, with another fitted smaller pot above it with a lid. This is used to melt chocolate or heat heavy cream and other ingredients that require low heat. You can use a bowl atop a pan if you do not have a double boiler and do not want to invest in one.
- ***Dry Measuring Cups**—Graduated cups for measuring flour and other dry ingredients.
- ***Electric Mixer**—I have written this book assuming that you have a four-quart electric stand-alone mixer. For small batches you may use a handheld electric mixer. I use and recommend KitchenAid mixers. It is worth the extra investment to get the slightly larger five-quart model.

- ***Grater**—A tool used to scrape or grate lemon, orange, and lime rind for fresh zest, which you will need for flavoring citrus cakes and fillings. It is also used for chocolate.
- ***Hot-Glue Gun**—An electric handheld tool used to glue things quickly. Glue sticks are fed into the gun and squeezed out. It's used for gluing the bottom tier of the cake onto the heavy base board. Glue guns are available at craft stores.
- ***Handheld Wire Whisk**—A metal tool used for mixing and whipping ingredients by hand.
- **Liquid Measuring Cups**—Usually Pyrex or plastic with handles or pouring spouts. You can get away with metal dry measuring cups if you do not have the Pyrex or plastic ones right away.
- ***Measuring Spoons**—Graduated spoons for measuring small amounts of spices, powders, and extracts.
- ***Oven Thermometer**—A gauge used for measuring the temperature of your oven.

  A Note about Ovens—Never rely on the built-in thermometer alone. Buy a small mercury thermometer mounted on a metal stand and put it in your oven to be sure. Always preheat your oven for fifteen to twenty minutes before starting to bake.

- ***Pans**—Six-, eight-, ten-, twelve-, and fourteen-inch aluminum pans, two inches in height, for baking cake layers. Two of each size.
- **Pastry Brush**—Used for spreading sugar syrup on the tops of cakes and for washing down the sides of your pan as you are cooking syrups.
- ***Sifter/Strainer**—A tool that has a fine screen for sifting flour and other dry ingredients. I often use a strainer with a fine mesh and a small triple sifter (a mechanical tool used to make your flour very fine. When you squeeze the handle, it passes a rotary blade across a fine metal screen for even, thorough sifting).
- ***Spatulas**—There are two types of spatulas: rubber, which are used for mixing, folding, and scraping the inside of a bowl or mixer, and metal, which are used for spreading frosting. You will need both. When buying metal spatulas, quality and size are important. I use two sizes and styles: one is a smaller offset spatula made of stainless steel with an eight-inch blade, while the other larger flat spatula has a

fourteen-inch blade with a wooden handle. The larger one is great for scraping and finishing the tops of larger tiers.
- ***Stainless-Steel Bowls**—Bowls of various sizes are necessary when making wedding cakes. Get the heavy-duty flat-bottomed type; a glass one comes in handy for microwaving.
- ***Waxed Paper or Parchment Paper**—Specially formulated paper for lining your cake pans. Parchment is slightly stronger, can be sketched on with pencil (unlike waxed paper), and is also useful for making paper decorating cones.

Specialty Products and Supplies

- **Fondant**—Also called sugar paste, it is a pliable frosting made with confectioners' sugar, gelatin, water, corn syrup, glycerin, and flavoring. It is rolled out and used to cover cakes and cut into shapes for decoration. You can make it or buy it. (Satin Ice Brand is used by many professionals, including me.)
- **Gum Paste**—Similar to fondant but dries harder and can be used to make very realistic looking flowers and figurines.
- **Premade Decorations**—Roses, leaves, and other icing flowers can be purchased for ease of decorating your cakes and are great to have on hand as backups.

Cake-Decorating Supplies

- ***Cake Stand**—A revolving stand for turning your cakes as you fill, frost, and decorate. Invest in a good heavy-duty metal turntable.
- **Clear Piping Gel**—A transparent gel that can be colored and is used to write on cakes and has other decorative uses.
- ***Couplers**—A plastic-screw attachment that is added to a pastry bag to make changing decorating tips easier.
- ***Decorating Tips**—Metal tubes with various openings for piping decorative edges, borders, flowers, and scrolls. The tips or tube fit over the coupler on a pastry bag.

- **Dragees Gold and Silver**—Various sized tiny balls made from sugar and colored either gold or silver. These are good to have on hand for quick decorations, especially on cupcakes.
- **Edible Glitter**—Various colored sugar sparkles used for decoration on cakes.
- ***Pastry Bags** (various sizes)—Also called piping bags, they are made from nylon or plastic. You will need at least two of these bags; twelve- and sixteen-inch sizes are good starters.
- **Paste Colors**—Special concentrated paste used for coloring frosting, fondant, and gum paste.
- **Parchment Triangles**—Paper precut in a triangle shape. These are handy for making a quick piping bag for small amounts of frosting and are also used for piping melted chocolate and royal icing.
- **Rose Nail**—A metal nail with a circular flat top used for making buttercream roses, also called flower nails.
- ***Scissors**—A good pair of scissors for cutting paper and for lifting flowers off a rose nail. No special brand of scissors is necessary.

Paper Products

- **Cake Boxes**—Boxes made for holding and transporting pastries and cakes. If you do a lot of cakes, it is worth buying them in bulk. You can purchase them individually at cake-supply and craft stores.
- ***Cardboard Rounds**—Also called cake disks, or cardboard cake circles, they are made to correspond with pan sizes and are necessary to place your cakes on when constructing a wedding cake.
- ***Cutters**—A good sharp pair of garden shears. These are used for cutting dowels to the exact height of a cake.
- ***Dowel Rods**—Long thin cylinders of wood with one pointed end, used to support cake tiers. Use them for larger or very heavy tiered cakes.
- ***Plastic Wrap and Unscented Plastic Bags**—Used to wrap the baked cakes for freezer or refrigerator storage.

- **Precut Parchment Circles**—Purchase these already cut to fit into your pans as lining when baking, or cut them yourself from a sheet of parchment. If you bake a lot of cakes, it is worth buying the precut circles.
- ***Straws**—Regular store-bought plastic drinking straws, used for doweling small tiered cakes.
- **Tuk N Ruffle**—Lacey decorative edging used to place around the base of a cake.
- ***Wedding-Cake Bases**—Foam, wooden, round supports or Masonite rounds. For a heavy wedding cake, fourteen inches or larger, use Masonite or wooden boards. Your local Home Depot, lumberyard, or hardware store can custom cut these for you. Boards should be cut four inches larger in diameter than the size of the bottom tier of the cake.

Baking and Cake-Decorating Terms

- **All-Purpose Flour**—Most commercial brands of all-purpose flour contain all-purpose flour (80 percent) and cake flour (20 percent) and are excellent for the cakes in this book.
- **Buttercream**—A frosting made from butter, confectioners' sugar, and flavoring. Another version is the Italian meringue buttercream, which incorporates a sweetened meringue into the butter and vanilla.
- **Cake Layers**—Each cake is made up of two or more horizontal slices of cake called layers.
- **Cake Tiers**—Each layered cake is a tier. Wedding cakes usually have graduated tiers sitting on top of one another—the largest cake at the bottom, a medium-sized one in the center, and a smaller one on top. Wedding cakes can have many tiers.
- **Creaming**—Creaming is a mixing method used to incorporate the maximum amount of air bubbles, held in by the fat, so a recipe will rise in the oven and be light in texture when baked.
- **Crumb Coating**—Also known as dirty icing, or first coat, crumb coating is a thin first layer of frosting that helps to keep the crumbs on the cake and not in the finished outer coat.
- **Dam**—A thick piped line of buttercream between two layers of cake. The dam helps to hold cake fillings in place and acts as a glue to hold the two layers of cake together.

- **Dry Ingredients**—Flour, sugar, baking powder, soda, salt, and so on. These are the dry ingredients of a recipe.
- **Egg-White Terms**—Whipping air into the whites of the egg is usually done with a small amount of sugar and cream of tartar. Stiff but not dry is when the whites will have tripled in volume and will hold their shape. If overwhipped they will become dry and difficult to fold into a batter or frosting. Shiny and firm (meringue) is obtained by whipping whites with a hot sugar syrup for use in buttercream.
- **Fold**—A gentle way to incorporate whipped egg whites or whipped cream into a batter or filling. Using a large rubber spatula, reach down through the center of the foam to the bottom of the bowl, and lift some of the batter up and on top of the foam. As you turn your wrist to deposit the batter on top of the eggs, you turn the bowl a few degrees. Repeat until all the egg-white foam or cream is incorporated.
- **Ice Bath**—A bowl of ice and water used to quickly cool down ingredients to bring it to the correct consistency—for example, to mend a frosting that is too soft.
- **Icing**—Technically a thin frosting that can be poured over a cake. Icing is sometimes used interchangeably with the term frosting.
- **Leveling**—A way of cutting a cake to assure that it is level. Special tools are available for this, or a good sharp serrated knife will do the job along with a level (the same type of level that a carpenter would use).
- **Piping**—Squeezing frosting out of a bag through special tips to make decorations or to write on cakes.
- **Royal Icing**—Primarily used for decorating and not for frosting a cake. Lace, fine lines and piping can be done over fondant cakes for a beautiful effect; also used to make flowers on wire to dry and place on cakes.
- **Separating Eggs**—To separate eggs, the first and most important step is to make sure your hands and equipment are free of grease. Use three small bowls. Crack the egg; transfer the egg yolk back and forth from one half of the shell to the other until the white of the egg separates into a bowl. Check for any yolk residue in your separated egg white. Discard it if there is. The tiniest amount of yolk or fat will prevent the whites from whipping to the full extent. Next place the yolk into a bowl, and finally transfer the white into the third bowl. Continue with the remaining eggs. Eggs should be at room temperature before use in cake batter.
- **Sifting**—Forcing dry ingredients, such as flour, through a screen to aerate and remove any lumps.

- **Unsalted Butter**—Also called sweet butter or sweet cream, this butter contains no salt.
- **Zest**—Is the colorful outer layer of a citrus fruit. To grate a lemon, lime, or orange, you will need a grater. Rub the citrus fruit along the grater to make a fine powder of the outer rind, being careful not to grate the white (bitter) part of the peel. The zest is used to flavor cakes, fillings, and frostings.

Illustration of Tiers and Layers

This illustration is to help you to distinguish between layers, tiers, and cakes. A wedding cake is comprised of tiers. Each tier commonly has two layers of cake with one layer of filling in between.

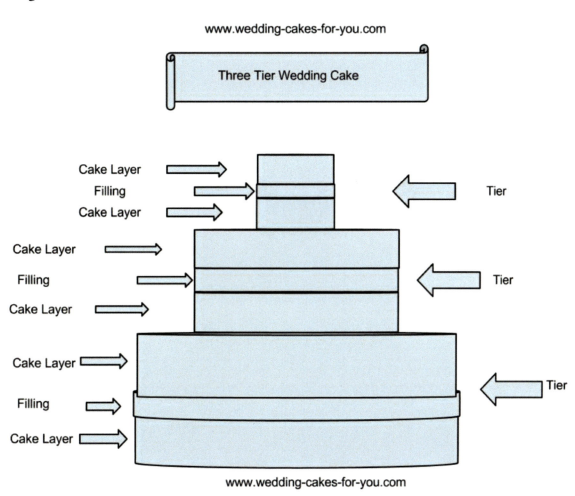

Baking Your Cakes

• • •

About Ovens

Ovens vary, and some will have hot spots. I recommend finding the true temperature of your oven in the center and on the sides with an oven thermometer. Another way to establish the variation in your oven is by observing how your cakes bake. Are they baking too quickly and then collapsing? Your oven needs to be turned down if that is the case. Are they browning unevenly? If yes, you may have to move your cakes around in the oven as they bake. I found that my oven does have hot spots and it was baking the cakes too quickly. I now bake all my cakes at 335 degrees Fahrenheit and move, spin, or switch the placement of them halfway through the baking process. When moving your cakes, be careful not to do it too soon, when the batter is still liquid. They may fall in the center if you jiggle them around or bump up against the racks. Wait until they start to bake in the center before attempting to pick them up and move them.

The wedding-cake sizes in the demonstration on the following pages are a three-tier cake with a twelve-inch bottom tier, a nine-inch center tier, and a six-inch top tier. This cake will serve seventy-five guests, the top tier going home with the bride and groom. The method shown is the same for larger cakes, with the exception of using wooden dowels. You can use plastic straws for smaller cakes and a wooden dowel through the center of the finished cake. (Doweling will be explained later). If you are making a larger cake, you may want to consider using Cake Stackers supports. Included with your book purchase is a discount coupon for Cake Stackers. To receive and use your coupon, go to http://www.wedding-cakes-for-you.com/bookcustomers.html.

Use this password to gain entry: c1a&k#e2s

Preparing Your Pans

Apply Crisco   Flour and line them with waxed paper

Apply Crisco with a paper towel (or a spray such as Pam or equivalent) onto the bottom and sides of your pans. Make sure that you coat them well.

Flour your pans starting with the smallest pan, working your way up to the largest. Put half a cup or so of flour into the six-inch pan. Swirl it around and tip it so that your pans are completely coated in flour, tap the excess into the next six-inch pan, and repeat and then tap the excess into the nine-inch pan until all the pans are floured.

Cut waxed paper to fit each pan. Place your pan on top of the waxed paper, and trace around it with a pen or use scissors to mark it. Cut the circles, and place them into your pans. For larger pans (such as a fourteen-inch size), you will need to cut two half circles and place them on the bottom of the pans.

Making Your Batter

For the demonstration cake, I used the vanilla wedding-cake recipe. You will need to multiply the original recipe times three. This will give you just enough batter. A four-quart mixer is used in this book to illustrate the method, assuming that most home bakers have a mixer of this size. Some of the videos and photos on the www.wedding-cakes-for-you.com website and on the Wedding Cakes For You YouTube channel show a twenty-quart mixer. If you have access to a larger mixer, you can mix your batter all at once. (Invest in a five-quart if possible; it will save you time and energy.) Go to the wedding-cake supplies page at http://www.wedding-cakes-for-you.com/weddingcakesupplies.html to see the model that I have recommended.

For this particular-size cake, make one batch times one and one batch times two.

TIMES ONE:
Batter for two 9-inch pans
3 cups sifted all-purpose flour: 13.5 ounces: 360 grams
1 tbsp. baking powder: ½ ounce: 14 grams
½ tsp. salt: ⅛ ounce: 6 grams
1 cup unsalted butter (2 sticks at room temperature): 8 ounces: 227 grams
2 cups granulated sugar: 14½ ounces: 412 grams
4 eggs (separated): grade A large
1 cup milk (or orange juice): 8¼ ounces: 235 grams
1 tsp. vanilla extract

TIMES TWO:
Batter for two 12-inch pans and two 6-inch pans
6 cups sifted all-purpose flour
2 tbsp. baking powder
1 tsp. salt
2 cup unsalted butter (4 sticks at room temperature)
4 cups granulated sugar
8 eggs (separated)
2 cup milk (or orange juice)
2 tsp. vanilla extract

You will need two large bowls and a sifter.

Start by sifting flour into one of your bowls. Measure the flour into the second bowl. Measure and sift the baking powder into the flour. Add salt and stir.

Start by sifting flour into one of the bowls

Measure the flour into the second bowl

Measure and sift the baking powder into the flour

Add salt and stir

Now in your four- or five-quart mixing bowl, put the butter and sugar, and beat them together until fluffy.

Separate the eggs. Make sure your hands and bowls are clean and free of grease. You will need three bowls. One bowl will be used exclusively for the individual egg whites. One bowl will be for your yolks. Once separated you can pour the single egg white into the third bowl. This is so you can check to make sure there are no traces of egg yolk in each white before adding it to the final bowl of whites. The egg whites will not beat properly if any oil from the yolks gets into them.

Add the egg yolks slowly to the butter and sugar mixture while continuing to mix at medium speed until it is well incorporated. Do not overmix the batter.

Add the sugar to the butter

Separate yolks from the whites of the eggs

Eggs are now separated

Add egg yolks to the butter and sugar mixture

Whip the whites. You may use a separate handheld mixer for this. Or if you have another four- or five-quart mixing bowl, you may use it. Whip the whites until stiff but not dry. The whites should hold their shape when the whip is lifted out of the bowl. Set aside.

The Final Steps: Starting and ending with the flour mix, add a third of the dry ingredients to the butter and sugar mixture. Alternate with the liquid (milk and vanilla or orange juice and vanilla), mixing well for about one minute after each addition and scraping the bowl occasionally. This whole process should take about four minutes.

Whip the white and set aside

Add the dry mixture alternately with liquid

NOTE: This amount of batter just fits into the four-quart mixer, with very little room to fold in the beaten egg whites. I recommend mixing the dry and wet together first in your four-quart mixer and then transferring the batter into a large bowl. You can now fold in the egg whites comfortably.

TIP: If you have a five-quart mixer, you may have room for the egg whites without having to transfer the batter to another bowl.

Liquid dry ingredients being added alternately with the dry

Add the egg whites into the batter in thirds

Fold the egg whites into the batter

Fold until there are no more streaks of egg white in the batter

Pour the batter into your prepared pans, and place them in the oven at 335–350 degrees Fahrenheit, depending on your oven, until golden and your cakes spring back when touched or a toothpick inserted into the center comes out clean.

Place your cakes into the preheated oven

Cakes are done when golden on top and spring back when pressed in the center

Removing Your Cakes from the Pans

When your cakes are cool enough to handle, place a cardboard round or cooling rack on the top of each cake and flip the cake over onto it. Peel off the waxed or parchment paper. Once the cakes are completely cooled, place another cardboard round (the same size as the cake) onto each cake and flip again. Your cakes will now be right side up. Remove the original cardboard round or cooling rack.

Step by Step

Place a cake rack or a cardboard round on top of the cake

Flip the cake over

After they are completely cooled, wrap your cakes (still on the cardboard rounds) in a plastic wrap, and place them in the refrigerator or freezer until you are ready to fill them. My recommendation is to place them in the freezer. Freezing preserves the freshness of your baked cakes (if they are well wrapped) and makes your cakes much easier to work with.

Peel off the waxed or parchment paper

Wrap the cakes in layers of plastic wrap

Method for freezing: Place each wrapped layer with its cardboard round in the freezer until it is solid. If you plan to keep your cakes frozen longer than two or three days, remove the prefrozen cakes from the freezer, stack them with their cardboard rounds, and wrap them in plastic, unscented clean garbage bags. Extract as much air as possible out of the bag. Return them to the freezer until you are ready to finish them.

Putting Your Cakes Together

• • •

Filling and Crumb Coating

Remove your cakes from the freezer or refrigerator, unwrap, and place one of the layers of your largest tier on the turntable. Pipe a one-inch dam of buttercream around the edge of the cake. You can use a large round or star tip for this. In the photos below, I used only a coupler without tips. Next place a mound of filling (in this case, buttercream) on top of the bottom tier. Spread that around evenly. Place the second layer on top and press gently. The buttercream dam acts as a glue to hold your cakes in place. Repeat for the rest of your cakes.

Pipe a dam of buttercream   Place filling in the center

Crumb coating your cake is important because it catches any loose crumbs and acts as a glue so that your finished cake will be crumb free. Follow the recipe for the Italian meringue buttercream. Take a generous amount of frosting, and place it on top of the filled cake. Spread the buttercream around and down onto the sides of the cake. This does not have to be neat; just coat the cake to hold all the crumbs in place. Scrape off any excess buttercream; this can be used to crumb coat the next tier, but since it may likely contain crumbs, it should not be used for finishing your cake.

Place the second layer on top

Place a generous amount of frosting on top and spread across the top and down the sides

Finished crumb coat

Wrap and refrigerate or freeze

Wrap and return your cakes to the refrigerator or freezer.

TIP: You can freeze your filled and crumb-coated cakes

Note: Use a long serrated cake knife to level the tops of the cakes, if you prefer, before you put them together. You may want to use a special leveling tool that is made by Wilton and can be purchased through the wedding-cake-decorating supplies page: http://www.wedding-cakes-for-you.com/weddingcakesupplies.html.

Frosting Your Cakes

If possible make your buttercream and fillings fresh and use them right away. This avoids having to thaw and rewhip later. However, if you do make your filling and frosting ahead, or if you fill and frost over a two- or three-day period, store it in airtight containers until you are ready to use it. Bring your buttercream to room temperature before rewhipping. Follow one of the frosting recipes in this book, and use the chart at the Customers only page as a guide to how much frosting you will need to fill and cover your cakes. http://www.wedding-cakes-for-you.com/bookcustomers.html.

Use this password to gain entry: c1a&k#e2s.

If your cakes are in the freezer, defrost them in the refrigerator. Once defrosted, remove your cakes from the refrigerator. Frost each cake separately, putting it on a turntable.

Optional: if the humidity is high and your crumb-coated cakes have beads of moisture on them, rough up the sides a little with an icing comb. This will give the frosting more grabbing power, helping it adhere to the cake better. If you do use a very cold cake, work quickly, as the butter in the frosting will harden fast. Once finished, you can place your cakes into the refrigerator until you are ready to decorate.

Start with your bottom tier. Pile the buttercream on top of the bottom tier. You will be scraping off any excess, so don't worry about putting on too much. Spread the icing to cover the top and then spin the turntable as you press gently so that the frosting hangs over the edges.

Add more frosting to the sides, and spread on a thick layer. At this point, do not try to make it smooth or pretty. Once you have the entire side thickly iced, start to scrape and turn the cake.

You might need to use a hot knife to make it super smooth depending on your final design. Repeat the procedure for each of your cakes.

Pile the buttercream on top

Spin the turntable as you spread the frosting around

Add more frosting to sides

Turn decorating table as you spread frosting to cover sides

TIP: To prevent the small six-inch cake from sliding around while frosting on the turntable, use a slightly damp cloth or towel under the cake or a piece of rubber shelf liner.

If this is your first cake, try using a design that does not require a smooth finish. Combing your cake is one way of making a pretty design. For a rustic look and an even simpler cake-decorating technique, run the spatula over the buttercream to make a natural shingles pattern or swirls. It's a very easy design for a beginner decorator or DIY (do it yourself) bride.

Use an up-and-down motion for a wavy effect

Comb straight with no up-and-down motion

Edging your cakes. Using your spatula, place it horizontally at the highest edge, and scrape it gently across the top (it takes practice to do this well). Most of the top part of each cake will not be visible once the cakes are stacked. You will also have a border to cover some imperfections around the edges, so you need not be overly concerned about making it perfect. You can also use the cake comb on the top to make a pattern.

Scrape the excess off the edges with a spatula

TIP: Fresh flowers around each tier can also be used to cover imperfections.

The Internal Structure of a Wedding Cake

This drawing illustrates the cardboard cake circles under each cake. The cardboard under the bottom or largest cake (tier) is glued onto the heavy wood or Masonite board. The smaller dowels inserted into each cake are cut to the height of each cake. They act as internal pillars or supports.

The center dowel is sharpened and cut to the height of the entire wedding cake. It is then inserted through all the cakes from top to bottom.

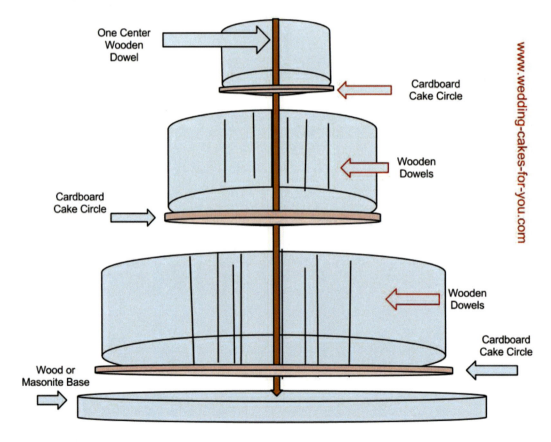

TIP: A solid base is important. Use silver foam Wilton cake bases or a Masonite or wooden board that has been custom cut.

Stacking Your Cakes

• • •

Using Dowels

STRAWS OR DOWELS HELP TO support the weight of cakes being stacked. Using a cake pan or bowl (as in the photo) as a marker, mark the bottom tier for placement of the dowels and the center tier. Now insert your sharpened dowels or straws, placing them evenly around the circle.

Using plastic straws is the simplest method and will work fine for a small wedding cake. If you want to use wooden dowels, you will need strong sharp cutters. You can buy Wilton precut and presharpened wooden dowels but will still need to trim them to size. Cut each dowel or straw the same length.

The bottom tier is hot glued to the cake base

Use your pans or bowl to mark the center of your cakes

Plastic straws or wooden dowels

Trim the straws or dowels

TIP: *A custom wooden board (covered in Fanci-foil, fondant, royal icing, or other decoration) can be used for heavier cakes so that the cake has a nice strong base. This will help to prevent the cold buttercream cakes from cracking when you move them and in general makes them more secure.*

After you place all your straws or dowels, sprinkle a small amount of coconut or graham-cracker crumbs onto the cake within the circle. This will prevent the tier above from sticking and pulling the buttercream away from the tier beneath it when the cake is cut and served.

Placement of straws or dowels

Sprinkle and spread graham-cracker crumbs within the marked circle

Step by Step

TIP: *An actual level can be used to check your cakes, but I have found that using a product called Cake Stacker's takes care of leveling and a few other issues that come up often with wedding cakes, such as centering your cakes and stress-free safe delivery.*

Place the second tier on top using the pan marks as a guide. Add the top tier to the middle tier, center it, measure, cut, and sharpen a wooden dowel and push it through the center of your entire cake.

- 12 dowels for a 14-inch cake
- 8 dowels for a 12-inch cake
- 6 dowels for an 8-inch cake

Place the middle tier on the bottom tier. Repeat marking and doweling. Place the top tier on the middle tier

A sharpened wooden dowel goes through the entire cake from top to bottom

DECORATING YOUR CAKES

To illustrate how you might decorate this three-tiered cake, I chose a rustic look, using a simple textured buttercream. This is a beautiful way to decorate a wedding cake and probably the simplest method for a DIY bride or if this is your first wedding cake. I share with you in my Wedding Cakes with Lorelie Step by Step companion video how I create this type of design on a cake using a spatula. Also included in the video is how to safely place fresh flowers onto a cake.

To see more design ideas and information on how to purchase the companion video, go to http://www.wedding-cakes-for-you.com/bookcustomers.html.

Use this password to gain entry: c1a&k#e2s.

Using Cake Stackers

Cake Stackers are an internal metal support system and can be used for a cake of any size. Large or tall cakes that are fourteen by ten by six and larger, whimsical upside-down and topsy-turvy designs are made much easier using this method of construction.

This system uses metal plates and metal dowels and works very much like the wooden dowels. Your cakes will be level and centered no matter what. Even if they are not level, the metal is thinner yet stronger and supports your cake perfectly.

I sometimes use this system because of the advantages over the wooden-dowel method. Delivery is safer; leveling and centering is guaranteed, and they really work.

Delivering Your Cakes

Getting your cake safely from one place to another can be challenging, especially if you will be traveling a long distance. The best solution I have found is a good sturdy box in which the base of the cake fits snugly. This will prevent your cake from shifting. The box is then taped, closed, and covered with plastic.

If you use a car for delivery, you can wedge your box between the seat and the dashboard using pads and pillows and a board under the cake box to keep it level. A van is the ideal vehicle for delivering, as you can put your boxed cake on a level floor. Make sure you arrange the box so it does not slide around in case of sudden stops.

> *TIP: If you are driving a long distance or if the weather is hot and/or humid, I suggest double boxing and using dry ice to make sure your cake stays cold.*

To see examples and photos of a real cake delivery and get access to your exclusive Cake Stackers coupon, go to wedding-cakes-for-you.com/bookcustomers.html.

Use this password to gain entry: c1a&k#e2s.

Lorelie's Best Recipes

• • •

Note about Measures: To obtain the grams and ounces for most of these recipes, I first measured with cups and spoons, using the dip-and-sweep method for dry ingredients, which is simply dipping the cup into the dry ingredient and then sweeping across the top with the straight edge of a spatula or knife. I followed this with weighing each ingredient on an electronic scale to obtain the equivalent in grams and ounces. The scaled ounces and grams may differ from what you may see with an online converter or in another book. Follow these exactly as they are written, and you will bake a perfect cake every time.

I converted the small-batch recipes to grams and ounces. You will find a chart at the end of each recipe with the recipes multiplied up to six times for you in cups. I have given you the base amounts for grams and ounces, and you can multiply those on your own as needed.

Each recipe begins with the original small-batch measurements with specific instructions to follow, the amount of batter the recipe produces, how much batter is needed per pan, how many times to multiply the recipe for various sized wedding cakes, advice and tips specific to that recipe, and the best combination of filling and frosting flavors to use.

Ingredients: The eggs in the recipes are US grade A large, weighing in at two ounces each with the shell. Butter is unsalted unless noted otherwise. Sugar is granulated unless noted otherwise. Flour is all-purpose, sifted and then measured unless noted otherwise. All ingredients should be at room temperature and weighed and measured before you begin mixing.

Batter-Amounts Chart: To make it easier to figure out the amount of batter you will need for wedding cakes...

Start by looking at the specific amount of batter the recipe makes. (I have provided that amount for you at the top of each recipe.)

Look at the typical wedding-cake configurations under each recipe, and choose one. There are many more combinations, but this will help you get started, and you can make your own combos from the ones provided.

Look at the chart to see how many times to multiply a recipe for each of the pan sizes you have chosen for your tiers, and add them up to estimate your ingredients for a full-size wedding cake. The chart is a printable provided for you at the Customers only special-access page on the website. Go to wedding-cakes-for-you.com/bookcustomers.html.

Use this password to gain entry: c1a&k#e2s.

Vanilla Cake

• • •

THE VANILLA-CAKE RECIPE IS MY go-to for a bride who wants a traditional cake that is moist and delicious and can go with just about any filling flavor. This cake is NOT pure white as it does contain egg yolks. If your bride insists on a snow-white cake, then I recommend the Simple Pure-White Cake recipe. The beauty of both these recipes is that you can use them as a base for many other flavors. I list some of those below for you. Use your unique ideas to add your own twist. This is the same recipe that I used in the demonstration cake in this book.

When making this or any other butter-based cake, keep in mind that it is best served at room temperature. The firmness of this recipe makes this a good choice for sculpting. The egg-white meringue that is folded into the batter at the end helps to add some lightness to the texture.

Preheat oven 335–350 degrees Fahrenheit

Cups of batter—5¾

Makes two-layer, each 8- or 9-inch, round cakes

Ingredients
3 cups sifted (then measured) all-purpose flour: 13.5 ounces: 360 grams
1 tbsp. baking powder: ½ ounces: 14 grams
½ tsp. salt: ⅛ ounce: 6 grams
1 cup butter softened: 8 ounces: 227 grams
2 cups granulated sugar: 14½ ounces: 412 grams
4 eggs separated: grade A large
1 cup whole milk: 8¼ ounces: 235 grams
1 tsp. vanilla

Method
Sift together flour, baking powder, and salt. Set aside.

In the large bowl of an electric mixer, beat the butter until soft and smooth. Add the sugar, and beat until light and smooth. Add egg yolks, one at a time, beating after each addition. Stop the mixer, and scrape down the sides of the bowl and the beaters several times.

With the mixer on low speed, alternately add the flour mixture and milk, beginning and ending with flour. Stir in the vanilla. At this point you may add flavoring touches if desired (orange zest, lemon zest, almond extract).

In another bowl, with a clean beater, beat the egg whites until stiff but not dry. Stir about half a cup of whites into the batter to lighten it, and then fold in remaining whites in several additions.

Divide the batter evenly between the pans. Smooth the batter level, and then spread it slightly from the center to the edges.

Bake in the preheated oven for thirty to thirty-five minutes or just until the tops are springy or a cake tester comes out clean.

Cool the cakes in their pans on a rack for ten minutes. Invert the cakes onto racks.

Batter Amounts and Multiplying the Vanilla-Cake Recipe

Listed below are some typical combinations for round pan sizes for wedding cakes and the number of times you will most likely need to multiply the recipe to make enough batter for your size of wedding-cake pans. If you have a large industrial mixer, you can most likely do one large batch. (I have a twenty-quart mixer and can do a wedding cake in one bowl for the most part). If you have a small mixer (four or five-quart bowl KitchenAid or equivalent), figure out how much batter will fit into your bowl and then how many batches you will need to reach the desired amount.

NOTE: Most but not all recipes multiplied by two can fit in a KitchenAid four- or five-quart mixer.

I have listed a few typical wedding-cake pan combinations to get you started. These are based on two-layer cakes and vary somewhat with each recipe. Keep your own notes on what works for you. Take into consideration the height of your pans and how much you wish to use, but remember that if you put too much batter in the pans, the cake may not bake properly.

These combinations include the six-inch top tier. Minus sixteen servings if the bride and groom will take home the cake top.

- Fourteen-ten-eight-six: serves 186—uses thirty-six cups of batter—× recipe by six or seven
- Fourteen-ten-six: serves 156—uses thirty-two cups of batter—× recipe by five or six

- Twelve-eight-six: serves 114—uses twenty-seven cups of batter—× recipe by four or five
- Ten-eight-six: serves 94—uses seventeen cups of batter—× recipe by three

Vanilla Cake Recipe Multiplied For You

X's	Flour	Baking Powder	Salt	Butter	Sugar	Eggs	Milk	Vanilla
2	6 cups	2 Tbls	1 tsp	2 cups	4 cups	8	2 cups	2 tsp
3	9 cups	3 Tbls	1 ½ tsp	3 cups	6 cups	12	3 cups	3 tsp
4	12 cups	4 Tbls	2 tsp	4 cups	8 cups	16	4 cups	4 tsp
5	15 cups	5 Tbls	2 ½ tsp	5 cups	10 cups	20	5 cups	5 tsp
6	18 cups	6 Tbls	3 tsp	6 cups	12 cups	24	6 cups	6 tsp

IDEAS AND SUGGESTIONS FOR THE VANILLA-CAKE RECIPE

- Almond—Substitute vanilla extract for almond extract, add little bit of ground almonds, and brush the cakes with amaretto. Suggested by Wedding Cakes For You website reader Amy Robertson
- Tropical Coconut—After you beat the butter and sugar together, add one cup of grated sweetened coconut, and substitute one teaspoon of coconut extract for the vanilla. Fill with coconut frosting.
- Luscious Lemon—Brush this lemony syrup over the cake layers. Syrup recipe—one-quarter to one-half cup of sugar and the juice of two lemons. Double or triple for a wedding cake, and fill the cake layers with English lemon curd mixed with buttercream. Add fresh raspberries for an especially fabulous flavor explosion.
- Orange Cake—Substitute milk for orange juice (optional: add the zest of one orange. Zest is the thin outer layer of the orange), and/or brush on Triple Sec or Grand Marnier over the layers. Raspberries and white-chocolate buttercream are especially delicious with the orange butter cake. This is my MOST requested flavor for a wedding cake. I always include this in a tasting, and it almost always wins out over the other flavors.
- Confetti Cake—Fold in along with the egg whites one-third cup of confetti or sprinkles to the recipe. Use whatever type confetti you like best. This adds a delightful crunch and color to the otherwise plain cake.

Almost any filling and frosting works for this cake. Some of the favorites are as follows:

- Chocolate mousse
- White-chocolate buttercream and raspberries
- Lemon buttercream
- Any flavor buttercream combination of your choice

This recipe has been a constant companion in my kitchen and for my brides for years, and it will probably become yours too.

Chocolate-Stout Cake

• • •

Recipe from Barrington Brew Pub with permission
Featured in *Bon Appetit* Magazine

I USED THIS AMAZING RECIPE for my sons wedding cake and covered it in fondant. The cake (photo above) sizes were fourteen by ten by eight by six inches, two layers each. This also makes a great grooms cake if the groom happens to be a Stout lover. There are many delicious flavored Stouts on the market so don't feel that you have to use Guinness as I did.

Preheat oven to 335–350 degrees Fahrenheit

Cups of batter: 8

Makes three-layer, each 8- or 9 inch-, round cakes

INGREDIENTS

2 cups stout (Guinness or other brand): 16 ounces: 460 grams
2 cups unsalted butter at room temperature: 16 ounces: 454 grams
1½ cups unsweetened cocoa powder: 2 ounces: 120 grams
4 cups all-purpose flour: 20 ounces: 560 grams
4 cups granulated sugar: 28 ounces: 800 grams
1 tbsp. baking soda
1½ tsp. salt
4 eggs, grade A large
1⅓ cups sour cream: 12 ounces: 326 grams
1 tsp. vanilla

METHOD

In a large heavy metal pot, bring the stout and the butter to a simmer in a heavy large saucepan over medium heat. Add cocoa powder, and stir till smooth. Let it cool slightly.

In another bowl whisk the flour, baking soda, sugar, and salt together. In the bowl of an electric mixer, beat the eggs and sour cream to blend. Add the stout chocolate mixture to the egg mixture, and beat just to combine. Add the flour mixture to the stout, chocolate, and egg mixture, and mix briefly on low speed.

Divide the batter evenly between the pans. Smooth the batter level, and then spread it slightly from the center to the edges.

Bake in the preheated oven for thirty to thirty-five minutes or just until the tops are springy or a cake tester comes out clean.

Batter Amounts and Multiplying the Chocolate-Stout Recipe

Listed below are some typical combinations for round pan sizes for wedding cakes and the number of times you will most likely need to multiply the recipe to make enough batter for your size of wedding-cake pans. If you have a large industrial mixer, you can most likely do one large batch. (I have a twenty-quart mixer and can do a wedding cake in one bowl for the most part). If you have a small mixer (four or five-quart bowl KitchenAid or equivalent), figure out how much batter will fit into your bowl and then how many batches you will need to reach the desired amount.

NOTE: Most but not all recipes multiplied by two can fit in a KitchenAid four- or five-quart mixer.

I have listed a few typical wedding-cake pan combinations to get you started. These are based on two-layer cakes and vary somewhat with each recipe. Keep your own notes on what works for you. Take into consideration the height of your pans and how much you wish to use, but remember that if you put too much batter in the pans, the cake may not bake properly.

These combinations include the six-inch top tier. Minus sixteen servings if the bride and groom will take home the cake top.

- Fourteen-ten-eight-six: serves 186—uses thirty-six cups of batter—× recipe by six
- Fourteen-ten-six: serves 156—uses thirty-two cups of batter—× recipe by five
- Twelve-eight-six: serves 114—uses twenty-seven cups of batter—× recipe by four
- Ten-eight-six: serves 94—uses seventeen cups of batter—× recipe by two

Chocolate Stout Cake Recipe Multiplied For You

X's	Stout	Butter	Cocoa	Flour	Sugar	Baking Soda	Salt	Eggs	Sour Cream	Vanilla
2	4 cups	4 cups	3 cups	8 cups	8 cups	2 Tbs	3 tsp	8	2 2/3 cups	2 tsp
3	6 cups	6 cups	4 ½ cups	12 cups	12 cups	3 Tbs	4 ½ tsp	12	4 cups	3 tsp
4	8 cups	8 cups	6 cups	18 cups	18 cups	4 Tbs	6 tsp	16	5 1/3 cups	4 tsp
5	10 cups	10 cups	7 ½ cup	20 cups	20 cups	5 Tbs	7 ½ tsp	20	6 2/3 cups	5 tsp
6	12 cups	12 cups	9 cups	24 cups	24 cups	6 Tbs	9 tsp	24	8 cups	6 tsp

IDEAS AND SUGGESTIONS FOR THE STOUT-CAKE RECIPE

Chocolate ganache is the original filling and frosting that goes with this cake recipe, but feel free to experiment with your own combinations. For a wedding cake like the one pictured above (my son's wedding cake), you can use a ganache filling as I did, with a buttercream of your choice and fondant.

TIP: If you are ever in Barrington, Massachusetts, you must visit the Barrington Brew Pub. The first thing you will see when you enter is this cake (four to five layers high) in a clear cake stand. It's a sight to see and a taste sensation that you don't want to miss.

MORE IDEAS

- Raspberry buttercream—Add raspberry puree to your favorite buttercream
- Buttercream
- White-chocolate buttercream
- Chocolate mousse

Chocolate-Buttermilk Cake

• • •

THIS IS MY ALL-TIME FAVORITE chocolate cake. It is made with vegetable oil instead of butter, which keeps it moist and fluffy even when it is cold. Buttermilk and strong coffee give it another step up, and it is super easy to make. I use this recipe a LOT. It appears that many visitors to the website along with their family, friends, and clients are also quite taken by this amazing chocolate cake. I use a blend of natural and dutched cocoa. The original recipe was on the back of a Hershey's Natural Cocoa container, so it was written specifically for the natural, but I think I have found the perfect combination of both worlds.

Preheat oven to 335–350 degrees Fahrenheit

Cups of batter: 5¾

Makes two-layer, 8- or 9-inch, round cakes

Ingredients

1¾ cups all-purpose flour: 7 ounces: 201 grams
2 cups granulated sugar: 14¾ ounces: 420 grams
¾ cups cocoa (I use SACO brand, which is a combination of natural and dutched process cocoa): 1 ounce: 60 grams
1½ tsp. baking soda
1½ tsp. baking powder
1 tsp. salt: ¼ ounce: 7 grams
1 cup buttermilk: 8 ounces: 230 grams
1 cup strong (liquid coffee): 8 ounces: 230 grams
½ cup oil: 4 ounces: 116 grams
2 eggs: grade A large
2 tsp. vanilla: ¼ ounce: 9 grams

TIP: Water can be used, but the coffee gives it a kick. Try using Turkish coffee if you like a strong flavor, or use instant if you don't feel like making a fresh pot.

Method

Measure out your ingredients, and place the dry ingredients into your mixing bowl. Give it a stir with your beater on low. Now add the wet ingredients to the dry, and mix on low to blend them together. Raise the beater speed to medium for a minute or so. Scrape the bowl and beater with a rubber spatula. Beat the mixture for two minutes.

Divide the batter evenly between the pans. Smooth the batter level, and then spread it slightly from the center to the edges.

Bake in the preheated oven for thirty to thirty-five minutes or just until the tops are springy or a cake tester comes out clean.

Cool the cakes in their pans on a rack for ten minutes. Invert the cakes onto racks.

Batter Amounts and Multiplying the Chocolate-Buttermilk Recipe

Listed below are some typical combinations for round pan sizes for wedding cakes and the number of times you will most likely need to multiply the recipe to make enough batter for your size of wedding-cake pans. If you have a large industrial mixer, you can most likely do one large batch. (I have a twenty-quart mixer and can do a wedding cake in one bowl for the most part). If you have a small mixer (four or five-quart bowl KitchenAid or equivalent), figure out how much batter will fit into your bowl and then how many batches you will need to reach the desired amount.

NOTE: Most but not all recipes multiplied by two can fit in a KitchenAid four- or five-quart mixer.

I have listed a few typical wedding-cake pan combinations to get you started. These are based on two-layer cakes and vary somewhat with each recipe. Keep your own notes on what works for you. Take into consideration the height of your pans and how much you wish to use, but remember that if you put too much batter in the pans, the cake may not bake properly.

These combinations include the six-inch top tier. Minus sixteen servings if the bride and groom will take home the cake top.

- Fourteen-ten-eight-six: serves 186—uses thirty-six cups of batter—× recipe by six or seven
- Fourteen-ten-six: serves 156—uses thirty-two cups of batter - × recipe by five or six
- Twelve-eight-six: serves 114—uses twenty-seven cups of batter—× recipe by four or five
- Ten-eight-six: serves 94—uses seventeen cups of batter—×recipe by three

Chocolate Cake Recipe Multiplied For You

X's	Flour	Sugar	Cocoa	B Soda	B Pow	Salt	Butter milk	Coffee	Oil	Eggs	Vanilla
2	3 ½ cups	4 cups	1 ½ cups	3 tsp	3 tsp	2 tsp	2 cups	2 cups	1 cup	4	4 tsp
3	5 ¼ cups	6 cups	2 ¼ cups	4.5 tsp	4.5 tsp	3 tsp	3 cups	3 cups	1 ½ cups	6	6 tsp
4	7 cups	8 cups	3 cups	6 tsp	6 tsp	4 tsp	4 cups	4 cups	2 cups	8	8 tsp
5	8 ¾ cups	10 cups	3 ¾ cups	7.5 tsp	7.5 tsp	5 tsp	5 cups	5 cups	2 ½ cups	10	10 tsp
6	10 ½ cups	12 cups	4 ½ cups	9 tsp	9 tsp	6 tsp	6 cups	6 cups	3 cups	12	12 tsp

IDEAS AND SUGGESTIONS FOR THE CHOCOLATE-CAKE RECIPE

The chocolate-buttermilk cake goes with so many fillings and frostings. Here are a few ideas:

- Chocolate ganache tastes incredible and holds the layers together
- Chocolate mousse is the one most of my brides choose to go with this cake
- Raspberry buttercream is awesome with chocolate. (Add raspberry preserves to taste to any buttercream recipe)
- Strawberry buttercream is a pleasant surprise filling. (Add strawberry preserves to taste to any buttercream recipe)
- Vanilla buttercream makes this cake taste like an Oreo cookie
- White-chocolate buttercream will take this to a new level

Another note about the chocolate-buttercream recipe: The batter is very thin. The cake will rise to the fullest if you don't overfill the pans. Sometimes you will see the batter bubble up in the center a bit. Do not get overly concerned if this happens. That center part can either be trimmed off or left as is. It seems that no matter what this cake comes out looking like, it always tastes fantastic.

This is my most requested recipe and goes well with plain old vanilla buttercream and lots of other fillings. I have also found that wedding guests are very pleasantly surprised to find a chocolate cake versus white cake. That may be because the white-cake experience over the years has not been a positive one. I guarantee if you use the vanilla cake or the simple white-cake recipe in this book, your clients and their guests will be beyond satisfied.

Prepare yourself for some great testimonials from your brides, family, and friends.

Carrot Cake

• • •

The very first wedding cake I ever made was a carrot cake. However it was not this tropical version. Even though it was a good one, this recipe is (in my opinion) the best. It takes a little more preparation, such as cooking and pureeing the carrots, processing the nuts, and draining the canned pineapple, to get most of the moisture out, but once that is finished and you have everything measured, it is very simple. **Here is a quick tip for you for this recipe.** Start cooking the carrots early in the day or even the day before so they can cool completely, and then process them in the food processor. You can freeze the puree if you must or if there are leftovers. Save it for the next carrot-cake order. Trust me, you will be getting a lot of carrot-cake orders if you add this to your cake tastings.

Preheat oven to 335–350 degrees Fahrenheit

Cups of batter: 8

Makes three-layer, each 8- or 9-inch, cakes (or two 10-inch thicker layers)

Ingredients
3 cups sifted (and then measured) all-purpose flour: 13½ ounces: 360 grams
3 cups granulated sugar: 1 lb. 5.5 ounces: 600 grams
1 tsp. salt: ¼ ounce: 7 grams
1 tbsp. baking soda
1 tbsp. cinnamon
1½ cups corn oil: 12 ounces: 290 grams
4 eggs: grade A large
1 tbsp. vanilla extract
1½ cups chopped walnuts (Process the walnuts in a food processor if possible. Be careful not to over process them or they will be more like a paste.): 6⅜ ounces: 181 grams
1½ cups shredded coconut: 4⅜ ounces: 127 grams
1⅓ cups cooked and pureed carrots (process the cooked carrots in a food processor or blender):10¾ ounces: 307 grams

NOTE: 2 lbs. of raw carrots boiled and pureed = 1 lb. 4 ounces or 573 grams. For this recipe times one starts with 1½ lbs. of raw carrots.

¾ cups crushed and well-drained pineapple (I use Dole brand, which comes in cans. Use the best brand possible or fresh if you want to do the work): 5 ounces: 164 grams

Method:
Mix together all the dry ingredients—flour, baking soda, salt, cinnamon, and sugar. Add oil, eggs, and vanilla; beat well, scraping the sides of the bowl a couple of times. Fold in the carrots, pineapple, coconut, and walnuts.

Divide the batter evenly between the pans. Smooth the batter level, and then spread it slightly from the center to the edges.

The baking time will vary depending on your oven. Bake in the preheated oven for thirty to thirty-five minutes or just until the tops are springy or a cake tester comes out clean.

Cool the cakes in their pans on a rack for ten minutes. Invert the cakes onto racks.

BATTER AMOUNTS AND MULTIPLYING THE CARROT-CAKE RECIPE

Listed below are some typical combinations for round pan sizes for wedding cakes and the number of times you will most likely need to multiply the recipe to make enough batter for your size of wedding-cake pans. If you have a large industrial mixer, you can most likely do one large batch. (I have a twenty-quart mixer and can do a wedding cake in one bowl for the most part). If you have a small mixer (four or five-quart bowl KitchenAid or equivalent), figure out how much batter will fit into your bowl and then how many batches you will need to reach the desired amount.

NOTE: Most but not all recipes multiplied by two can fit in a KitchenAid four- or five-quart mixer.

I have listed a few typical wedding-cake pan combinations to get you started. These are based on two-layer cakes and vary somewhat with each recipe. Keep your own notes on what works for you. Take into consideration the height of your pans and how much you wish to use, but remember that if you put too much batter in the pans, the cake may not bake properly.

These combinations include the six-inch top tier. Minus sixteen servings if the bride and groom will take home the cake top.

- Fourteen-ten-eight-six: serves 186—uses thirty-six cups of batter—x recipe by five
- Fourteen-ten-six: serves 156—uses thirty-two cups of batter—x recipe by four

- Twelve-eight-six: serves 114—uses twenty-seven cups of batter—× recipe by three
- Ten-eight-six: serves 94—uses seventeen cups of batter—× recipe by two

The Carrot Cake Recipe Multiplied For You

X's	Flour	Sugar	Salt	Bake Soda	Cinnamon	Corn Oil	Eggs	Vanilla	Walnuts	Coconut	Carrot	Pineapple
2	6 cups	6 cups	2 tsp	2 Tbs	2 Tbs	3 cups	8	2 Tbs	3 cups	3 cups	2 2/3 cups	1 ½ cups
3	9 cups	9 cups	3 tsp	3 Tbs	3 Tbs	4 ½ cups	12	3 Tbs	4 ½ cups	4 ½ cups	4 cups	2 ¼ cups
4	12 cups	12 cups	4 tsp	4 Tbs	4 tbs	6 cups	16	4 Tbs	6 cups	6 cups	5 1/3 cups	3 cups
5	15 cups	15 cups	5 tsp	5 Tbs	5 Tbs	7 ½ cups	20	5 Tbs	7 ½ cups	7 ½ cups	6 1/3 cups	3 ¾ cups

Ideas and suggestions for the carrot-cake recipe

I have found that the best filling for this cake is the lemon cream-cheese frosting and/or lemon buttercream.

> TIP: To fill a full-sized carrot wedding cake with cream-cheese frosting (fourteen by ten by eight by six size, recipe × five), you will need two and a half pounds of cream cheese, one pound of butter (unsalted), fifteen cups of confectioner's sugar, juice of two lemons, and four teaspoons of vanilla.

This cake and all the cakes in this book freeze very well. Cool and wrap the cakes in layers of plastic wrap for up to a week or cool the cakes, fill, crumb coat, wrap, and freeze until ready to finish.

Best outer layer of frosting to use for this cake is buttercream. Cream-cheese icing tends to be slightly opaque. To give the cake more cream-cheese flavor, use the cream-cheese icing as a crumb coat or mix half and half (buttercream and cream-cheese frosting to use as a crumb or finishing coat).

More unique fillings: I find chocolate and caramel goes nicely with the carrot cake.

- Chocolate ganache
- Chocolate mousse
- Caramel filling
- White-chocolate buttercream

Hazelnut Cake

• • •

This is a special cake that my girlfriend requested for her wedding day twenty-five years ago. Many of my website visitors asked for a hazelnut recipe, so I dug this one out of the archives. It is unique and quite delicious as it is light in texture, very moist, and has a wonderful and unique aroma. I was thrilled to bring it back to life, as the recipe had sat in my recipe collection for a very long time. It will probably be rare that a bride will ask for this, but I can almost guarantee if you use this recipe for a tasting, you will receive orders. I think this cake would be fabulous as dessert for a holiday feast or other family gathering, especially if you have a gourmet-food lover in the family.

Please read through this entire recipe first.

Makes two-layer, each 9- or 10-inch, cakes

Ingredients

½ lb. of hazelnuts roasted and then ground to equal ¾ cups packed: 2 ounces: 84 grams *(see the note below about preparing hazelnuts or substituting with hazelnut meal)*
2 cups all-purpose flour: 9½ ounces: 272 grams
1½ tsp. baking soda
¼ tsp. salt
¾ cups unsweetened cocoa powder: 2 ounces: 60 grams
¾ cups boiling water: 6 ounces: 178 grams
1½ sticks unsalted butter softened: 6 ounces: 172 grams
1½ cups (packed) brown sugar: 8⅞ ounces: 249 grams
1 cup granulated sugar: 7 ounces: 200 grams
4½ eggs (room temp): 6.75 ounces: 158 grams
1 tbsp. vanilla extract
1½ cups buttermilk (room temp): 12 ounces: 345 grams

NOTE: You can choose to substitute the fresh hazelnuts with three-quarter cups hazelnut meal. Or prepare the hazelnuts up to a week in advance and store them tightly covered in the freezer.

If you choose to prepare your own nuts, then follow step one below.

Preheat oven to 325 degrees Fahrenheit.

1. Spread hazelnuts on a baking sheet, and roast until some of the skins are cracked and nuts are fragrant, about ten minutes. In batches, rub the warm nuts in a kitchen towel to remove as much of the dark-brown skin as possible. Let them cool.

Transfer the nuts to a food processor, and process until finely ground, but not pasty, for about twenty seconds.

Set aside three-quarter cups (packed) of the ground nuts.

Increase the oven temperature to 335–350 degrees Fahrenheit

Cups of batter: 8

Method

In a medium bowl, toss together the flour, baking soda, salt, and ground hazelnuts. Set aside.

In a heatproof bowl or large measuring cup, whisk together the cocoa and boiling water until smooth. (This will thicken as it cools).

In a large mixing bowl, beat the butter with a handheld mixer until fluffy, about two minutes. Add the brown sugar, and beat on high speed for three minutes. Add the granulated sugar, and beat on high speed for three more minutes. Add the eggs one at a time, and beat on medium speed until blended. Mix in the vanilla.

Gradually add the cooled cocoa paste at low speed and mix, scraping down the sides of the bowl if necessary until blended. On low speed, alternately add the buttermilk and the flour mixture in three additions, beginning and ending with the flour mixture. Continue to beat on medium-high speed until smooth, about one minute. (The batter may appear slightly curdled from the buttermilk). Transfer the batter to the prepared pans, filling each one about two-thirds full.

Place the pans into the oven, and bake until firm to the touch. Keep a close watch.

Batter Amounts and Multiplying the Hazelnut-Cake Recipe

Listed below are some typical combinations for round pan sizes for wedding cakes and the number of times you will most likely need to multiply the recipe to make enough batter for your size of wedding-cake pans. If you have a large industrial mixer, you can most likely do one large batch. (I have a twenty-quart mixer and can do a wedding cake in one bowl for the most part). If you have a small mixer (four or five-quart bowl KitchenAid or equivalent), figure out how much batter will fit into your bowl and then how many batches you will need to reach the desired amount.

NOTE: Most but not all recipes multiplied by two can fit in a KitchenAid four- or five-quart mixer.

I have listed a few typical wedding-cake pan combinations to get you started. These are based on two-layer cakes and vary somewhat with each recipe. Keep your own notes on what works for you. Take into consideration the height of your pans and how much you wish to use, but remember that if you put too much batter in the pans, the cake may not bake properly.

These combinations include the six-inch top tier. Minus sixteen servings if the bride and groom will take home the cake top.

- Fourteen-ten-eight-six: serves 186—uses thirty-six cups of batter—× recipe by five to six.
- Fourteen-ten-six: serves 156—uses thirty-two cups of batter—× recipe by three to four
- Twelve-eight-six: serves 114—uses twenty-seven cups of batter—× recipe by two to three
- Ten-eight-six: serves 94—uses seventeen cups of batter—× recipe by two

The Hazelnut Cake Recipe Multiplied For You

X's	Flour	Baking Soda	Salt	Cocoa Powder	Water	Butter	Brown Sugar	Sugar	Eggs	Buttermilk	Vanilla	Hazelnuts
2	4 cups	3 tsp	½ tsp	1 ½ cups	1 ½ cups	3 sticks	3 cups	2 cups	9 or 13.5 ounces	3 cups	2 Tbs	1 lb or 1 ½ cups
3	6 cups	4 ½ tsp	¾ tsp	2 ¼ cups	2 ¼ cups	4 ½ sticks	4 ½ cups	3 cups	13.5 or 20.25 ounces	4 ½ cups	3 Tbs	1 ½ lbs. 2 ¼ cups
4	8 cups	6 tsp	1 tsp	3 cups	3 cups	6 sticks	6 cups	4 cups	18 or 1 lb. 7 ounce	4 ½ cups	4 Tbs	2 lbs or 2 ½ cups
5	10 cups	7 ½ tsp	1 ¼ tsp	3 ¾ cups	3 ¾ cups	7 ½ sticks	7 ½ cups	5 cups	22 ½ or 2 lbs. 10 ounce	7 ½ cups	5 Tbs	2 ½ lbs. or 3 ¼ cups
6	12 cups	9 tsp	1 ½ tsp	4 ½ cups	4 ½ cups	9 sticks	18 cups	6 cups	27 or 2 lbs 53 ounce	9 cups	6 Tbs	3 lbs. or 4 ½ cups

Ideas and suggestions for the hazelnut-cake recipe

This is a very subtle soft-textured cake that goes well with a soft filling, but it is also possible that a chocolate ganache would be a delicious addition. It would also help to give the cake more structure for a wedding cake.

- Whipped cream fillings—Add almond extract and hazelnut meal for texture and flavor
- Chocolate ganache
- Chocolate mousse

Simple Pure-White Cake

• • •

If you are searching for the perfect pure-white cake for your bride's cake, this is it! This white-cake recipe may be simple, but the result is the fluffiest, most delicious white cake I personally have EVER made. Try it! This may become your go-to recipe for white cake. You can add variety by changing the flavor extract (I use almond) or by adding chopped nuts or coconut and by changing the frosting and filling. I used Swiss meringue buttercream, which makes the perfect bride's cake.

Preheat oven to 335–350 degrees Fahrenheit

Cups of batter: 5¾

Makes two-layer, each 8- or 9-inch, cakes

Ingredients

2 cups all-purpose flour: 8.5 ounces: 240 grams
1½ cups granulated sugar: 10.5 ounces: 300 grams
1 tbsp. baking powder
½ tsp. salt
1 cup milk: 8 ounces: 230 grams
½ cup shortening: 3 ounces: 89 grams
1 tsp. vanilla or almond extract
Egg whites from 5 grade A large eggs

Method

Place the flour, sugar, baking powder, salt, milk, and shortening in a mixing bowl and blend at low speed until it is moistened. Increase the speed to medium and beat for two minutes. Add the egg whites and flavoring and beat for another two minutes. Pour into greased and floured (and optional waxed paper lining) eight- or nine-inch pans and bake for 25–35 minutes or until done. It is done when it springs back to the touch or a toothpick inserted in center comes out clean.

Batter Amounts and Multiplying the Simple White-Cake Recipe

Listed below are some typical combinations for round pan sizes for wedding cakes and the number of times you will most likely need to multiply the recipe to make enough batter for your size of wedding-cake pans. If you have a large industrial mixer, you can most likely do one large batch. (I have a twenty-quart mixer and can do a wedding cake in one bowl for the most part). If you have a small mixer (four or five-quart bowl KitchenAid or equivalent), figure out how much batter will fit into your bowl and then how many batches you will need to reach the desired amount.

NOTE: Most but not all recipes multiplied by two can fit in a KitchenAid four- or five-quart mixer.

I have listed a few typical wedding-cake pan combinations to get you started. These are based on two-layer cakes and vary somewhat with each recipe. Keep your own notes on what works for you. Take into consideration the height of your pans and how much you wish to use, but remember that if you put too much batter in the pans, the cake may not bake properly.

These combinations include the six-inch top tier. Minus sixteen servings if the bride and groom will take home the cake top.

- Fourteen-ten-eight-six: serves 186—uses thirty-six cups of batter—× recipe by six or seven
- Fourteen-ten-six: serves 156—uses thirty-two cups of batter—× recipe by five or six
- Twelve-eight-six: serves 114—uses twenty-seven cups of batter—× recipe by four or five
- Ten-eight-six: serves 94—uses seventeen cups of batter—× recipe by three

Pure White Cake Multiplied For You

X's	Flour	Sugar	Baking Powder	Salt	Milk	Shortening	Vanilla	Egg Whites
2	4 cups	3 cups	2 Tbs	1 tsp	2 cups	1 cup	2 tsp	10
3	6 cups	4 ½ cups	3 Tbs	1 ½ tsp	3 cups	1 ½ cups	1 Tbs	15
4	8 cups	6 cups	4 Tbs	2 tsp	4 cups	2 cups	1 Tbs plus 1 tsp tsp	20
5	10 cups	7 ½ cups	5 Tbs	2 ½ tsp	5 cups	2 ½ cups	1 Tbs plus 2 tsp	25
6	12 cups	9 cups	6 Tbs	3 tsp	6 cups	3 cups	2 Tbs	30

IDEAS AND SUGGESTIONS FOR THE PURE-WHITE-CAKE RECIPE

- White-chocolate buttercream
- Italian meringue frosting
- Chocolate mousse
- Raspberry mousse
- Lemon filling—your favorite buttercream combined with lemon curd

Coconut Cake

• • •

The coconut cake is truly my NEW all-time favorite. Coupled with a pineapple or lemon filling, it is incredible. I began making this recipe recently as I had a special request for it and I wanted to try a newer version than the one I was using. This one won me over big time. The cake photo above was made using this coconut-cake recipe with a cream-cheese-and-pineapple filling. It was a HUGE hit. Since then I have made it many times over with perfect results.

Preheat oven to 335–350 degrees Fahrenheit

Cups of batter: 5

Makes two- or three-layer, each 8- or 9-inch, round cakes

Ingredients

2¾ cups of sifted cake flour: 10⅝ ounces: 301 grams
1 tsp. baking powder
½ tsp. baking soda
½ tsp. salt
½ cup of butter: 4 ounces: 115 grams
1¾ cups of granulated sugar: 12¾ ounces: 361 grams
1 cup cream of coconut (Coco Lopez Brand): 10½ ounces: 300 grams
1 cup buttermilk: 8 ounces: 230 grams
½ tsp. vanilla
½ tsp. coconut extract
4 eggs: grade A large

Method

Have the eggs at room temperature (you can warm them in warm water to for about five minutes if needed). Separate the whites and the yolks. Transfer them to another bowl, and set aside.

Cream the softened unsalted butter with the granulated sugar and the canned cream of coconut. Mix on medium-high speed for about three minutes or until the mixture is lighter, scraping the bowl a couple of times during the process.

NOTE: Do not use coconut milk.

Test the sugar and butter mixture for doneness by rubbing a little between your fingertips. It will still feel slightly gritty. Add the egg yolks one at a time mixing well after each addition. Once the yolks are mixed, add vanilla and coconut extracts, and mix at low speed. Sift the flour, baking powder, baking soda, and salt together onto a piece of waxed paper or into a bowl.

Add the flour mixture to the butter mixture on low speed. Add one cup of buttermilk. Increase the speed, and beat for a few seconds until the flour and buttermilk are incorporated.

Put the egg whites into a clean beater bowl. Beat them with a pinch of salt until stiff but not dry.

Fold the egg whites into the batter.

Split the batter between three eight- or nine-inch round pans, and bake for fifteen to twenty minutes. Or you may use two eight- or nine-inch pans and bake a little longer.

Batter Amounts and Multiplying the Coconut-Cake Recipe

Listed below are some typical combinations for round pan sizes for wedding cakes and the number of times you will most likely need to multiply the recipe to make enough batter for your size of wedding-cake pans. If you have a large industrial mixer, you can most likely do one large batch. (I have a twenty-quart mixer and can do a wedding cake in one bowl for the most part). If you have a small mixer (four or five-quart bowl KitchenAid or equivalent), figure out how much batter will fit into your bowl and then how many batches you will need to reach the desired amount.

NOTE: Most but not all recipes multiplied by two can fit in a KitchenAid four- or five-quart mixer.

I have listed a few typical wedding-cake pan combinations to get you started. These are based on two-layer cakes and vary somewhat with each recipe. Keep your own notes on what works for you. Take into consideration the height of your pans and how much you wish to use, but remember that if you put too much batter in the pans, the cake may not bake properly.

These combinations include the six-inch top tier. Minus sixteen servings if the bride and groom will take home the cake top.

- Fourteen-ten-eight-six: serves 186—uses thirty six cups of batter—×recipe by six or seven

- Fourteen-ten-six: serves 156—uses thirty-two cups of batter—× recipe by five or six
- Twelve-eight-six: serves 114—uses twenty-seven cups of batter—× recipe by four or five
- Ten-eight-six: serves 94—uses seventeen cups of batter—× recipe by three

The Coconut Cake Recipe Mulitplied For You

X's	Flour	Baking Powder	Baking Soda	Salt	Butter	Sugar	Cream of Coconut	Butter milk	Vanilla	Coconut Extract	Eggs
2	5 ½ cups	2 tsp	1 tsp	1 tsp	1 cup	3 ½ cups	2 cups	2 cups	1 tsp	1 tsp	8
3	8 ¼ cups	3 tsp	1 ½ tsp	1 ½ tsp	1 ½ cups	5 ¼ cups	3 cups	3 cups	1 ½ tsp	1 ½ tsp	12
4	11 cups	4 tsp	2 tsp	2 tsp	2 cups	7 cups	4 cups	4 cups	2 tsp	2 tsp	16
5	13 ¾ cups	5 tsp	2 ½ tsp	2 ½ tsp	2 ½ cups	8 ¾ cups	5 cups	5 cups	2 ½ tsp	2 ½ tsp	20
6	16 ½	6 tsp	3 tsp	3 tsp	3 cups	10 ½ cups	6 cups	6 cups	3 tsp	3 tsp	24

IDEAS AND SUGGESTIONS FOR THE COCONUT-CAKE RECIPE

I have two personal favorites for filling this cake and I choose to mix them into one. The pineapple filling alone is slightly risky. It is a bit slippery like lemon curd so I pair it with the frosting and that is incredible. The same can be done with lemon curd, which is also amazing with this recipe.

- Fresh-pineapple filling mixed with coconut cream-cheese frosting
- Lemon curd mixed with coconut cream-cheese frosting

Find Coco Lopez online if you can't find it in your local store. Or you can try another brand of cream of coconut. Coco Lopez®, La Preferida®, and Pepe Lopez® are the three top brands. Look in the section in your grocery store where they sell drink mixers or in a store where liquor is sold. Cream of coconut is used to make tropical drinks such as piña colada.

TIP: Substitute for cake flour and all-purpose flour. To make cake flour, substitute two tablespoons cornstarch for two tablespoons of flour in every cup. To substitute cake flour for all-purpose flour, use one cup plus two tablespoons cake flour for every cup.

To see and print out the charts for pan sizes, serving, and batter amounts, go to http://www.wedding-cakes-for-you.com/bookcustomers.html.

Use this password to gain entry: c1a&k#e2s.

Chocolate Ganache

• • •

FILLS TWO-LAYER NINE- OR TEN-INCH cakes with leftovers

This cooked chocolate icing can be used as a glaze while still warm, or as it cools down, it becomes a wonderful rich filling or dark-chocolate icing. This is especially good with the chocolate cake but can be used for all three of the top wedding-cake recipes, including the carrot cake for an exotic flavor.

TIP: Completely cooled, it can be shaped into balls and rolled into coconut or chopped nuts to make a delicious candy.

INGREDIENTS
2 cups heavy cream: 16 ounces: 460 grams
16 ounces Ghirardelli chocolate or a high-quality semisweet or bittersweet chocolate: 427 grams
Optional: 3 tablespoons of corn syrup to make the ganache shiny when using as glaze
Optional: 1 tsp. of flavoring or liqueur

METHOD
Heat the cream over low heat. Add the chocolate, and stir until melted and incorporated into the cream.

The mixture will go from milky to dark and smooth.

The frosting will get thicker as it cools.

Chocolate Ganache for a Wedding Cake

Fills a two-layer fourteen-, ten-, eight-, and six-inch wedding cake

Ingredients

6 cups heavy cream
48 ounces Ghirardelli chocolate or a high-quality semisweet or bittersweet chocolate
Optional 9 tablespoons corn syrup to make the ganache shiny when using as glaze.
Optional 3 tsp. flavoring or liqueur

Follow the method above.

> TIP: Ganache changes quickly from liquid to semisolid. If you are planning on using it for a filling, you will need to watch it carefully as it cools and use it as soon as it reaches the proper consistency. You may heat it in a bowl over warm water or cool it in a bowl over ice if needed.

Chocolate Mousse

• • •

Fills a two-layer eight- or nine-inch cake with leftovers, or one twelve-inch cake

Ingredients
6 ounces chocolate—semisweet or bittersweet: 171 grams
1 stick unsalted butter: 4 ounces: 113 grams
3 eggs, separated, at room temperature: grade A large
2 tbsp. sugar
¾–1 cup heavy cream (Use 1 cup for added lightness): 8 ounces: 235 grams
½ tsp. vanilla

Method
Melt the chocolate with the butter in a double boiler or hot water, being careful not to get steam into the chocolate mixture. Stir as you are melting it; remove from the heat to cool.

Separate the eggs. Set the whites aside.

Add the egg yolks one at a time to the cooled mixture and blend.

Place the whites in a clean bowl, and whip with one tablespoon of the sugar to medium-soft peaks.

In another bowl whip the heavy cream with one tablespoon of sugar and the vanilla. Beat until the cream holds its shape.

Fold the cream into the chocolate, but do not overmix. You should stop before it's fully mixed.

Next fold in the whites carefully. Again, do not overmix. You will see streaks of the cream and the egg whites in the chocolate. If you overmix, it starts to break down and becomes a gooey, ugly mess.

For best results, use it right away to fill your cooled cakes, and immediately put your cakes into the refrigerator or freezer to get firm. (The butter in this recipe helps to make it firm when cooled.)

Be careful not to overwork the mousse when you put it on your cake layer. Be gentle with it. You want it to remain fluffy and light.

Chocolate Mousse for a Wedding Cake
Fills a two-layer fourteen-, ten-, eight-, and six-inch wedding cake

Ingredients
18 ounces chocolate—semisweet or bittersweet.
3 sticks unsalted butter (12 ounces)
9 eggs, separated, at room temperature
6 tbsp. sugar
2¼–3 cups heavy cream (I use 3 for added lightness)
1½ tsp. vanilla

Method
Melt the chocolate with the butter in a double boiler or hot water, being careful not to get steam into the chocolate mixture. Stir as you are melting it; remove from the heat to cool.

Separate the eggs. Set the whites aside.

Add the egg yolks one at a time to the cooled mixture and blend.

Place the whites in a clean bowl, and whip with three tablespoons of the sugar to medium-soft peaks.

In another bowl whip the heavy cream with three tablespoons of sugar and the vanilla. Beat until the cream holds its shape.

Fold the cream into the chocolate, but do not overmix. You should stop before it's fully mixed.

Next fold in the whites carefully. Again, do not overmix. You will see streaks of the cream and the egg whites in the chocolate. If you overmix, it starts to break down and becomes a gooey, ugly mess.

For best results, use it right away to fill your cooled cakes, and immediately put your cakes into the refrigerator or freezer to get firm. (The butter in this recipe helps to make it firm when cooled.) Be careful not to overwork the mousse when you put it on your cake layer. Be gentle with it. You want it to remain fluffy and light.

> *TIP: The chocolate mousse filling is best when used immediately after making it. Put it between the layers, crumb coat, and then freeze or chill your cakes.*

Lemon Cream Cheese

• • •

Fills a nine- or ten-inch cake

This recipe is simple and delicious. It goes well with either the carrot-cake recipe or the chocolate-cake recipe. Make sure the cream cheese and the butter are at room temperature before mixing.

Ingredients
8 ounces cream cheese: 230 grams
6 tbsp. unsalted butter: 3 ounces: 81 grams
3 cups confectioners' sugar (or to taste): 13 ounces: 372 grams
1 tsp. vanilla extract
Juice of ½ lemon (optional)

Method
Cream together cream cheese and butter in a mixing bowl. Slowly sift in the confectioners' sugar, and continue beating until fully incorporated. Mixture should be free of lumps. Stir in vanilla and lemon.

Lemon Cream-Cheese Filling for a Wedding Cake
Fills and crumb coats fourteen-, ten-, eight-, and six-inch cakes

If you don't have a large mixer, you will need to do this in smaller batches.

Ingredients
2½ lbs. cream cheese
1 lb. butter
15 cups confectioners' sugar
Juice of 2 lemons
3 tbsp. plus 1 tsp. vanilla

Method
Cream together cream cheese and butter in a mixing bowl. Slowly sift in the confectioners' sugar and continue beating until fully incorporated. Mixture should be free of lumps. Stir in the vanilla and lemon.

> *TIP: Add the lemon at the very end of the mixing process. Cream-cheese frosting is OK for crumb coating but not recommended for a final coat. Use buttercream for a smoother finish.*

Italian Meringue Buttercream

● ● ●

Enough for a fourteen-, ten-, and six-inch wedding cake). You will need more for a basket-weave cake or a cake with lots of buttercream roses, leaves, and other embellishments.

If you have a small mixer, you will need to cut this in half and do two batches. To save time, cook the full amount of sugar, and then split into two equal parts.

Ingredients
4 lbs. unsalted butter at room temperature: 1.873 kilograms
1 cup water: 8 ounces: 230 grams
2¼ cups sugar plus 6 tbsp.
9 egg whites at room temperature: grade A large
Vanilla to taste
Optional: pinch of salt

Method
Whip the butter until it is as light and fluffy as possible. Add vanilla and, if needed, salt. Set aside.

Alternate Method: Chop the butter into small pieces, and set aside.

Next place the water and sugar into a pot, and cook until the temperature reaches 238 degrees Fahrenheit. As the mixture is cooking, occasionally sweep the edges of the pot with a pastry brush dipped in water. This will help to prevent crystals from forming.

Whip the egg whites in a clean bowl with clean beaters until soft peaks form.

Slowly add the hot syrup to the whipped egg whites. Mix the egg whites and syrup until the whites are shiny and the peaks are firm. It will be like the consistency of marshmallow.

Slowly add bits of the room-temperature butter (chunks or prewhipped) to the egg whites and sugar. It will appear not to mix very well at first; in fact it may look a little curdled, but it will come together and be very smooth and creamy in the end.

If you used the chopped butter method, add the vanilla at the end.

You can store this buttercream well-covered in the refrigerator for a couple of weeks. When you are ready to use it again, let it come to room temperature before rewhipping.

TIP: Remove the water and sugar (also called syrup) a degree or two before it reaches 238 degrees Fahrenheit, as it will continue to cook when you remove it from the stove top. Have the egg whites prewhipped and use it right away.

English Lemon Curd for Flavoring Buttercream

If you want to make your lemon buttercream special, use this English lemon curd to flavor your buttercream.

Ingredients
4 egg yolks: grade A large
1 cup sugar: 8 ounces: 230 grams
12 tbsp. lemon juice (¾ cup): 5¾ ounces: 161 grams
4 tsp. lemon zest (2 lemons)
8 ounces unsalted butter: 226 grams

Method
Start by zesting and straining your lemons. Use a simple lemon juicer.

You may have to strain the tiny lemon seeds out. Place the egg yolks into a pan. Add the sugar, strained lemon juice, and lemon zest. Mix it together thoroughly.

Cook over low heat stirring constantly until the mixture starts to thicken.

Cook for a couple of minutes, and check to see if it's done. It will coat the back of a wooden or metal spoon if it is done.

Put the finished curd into a bowl (nonmetallic). Poke a few holes in a piece of plastic wrap, and lay it right onto the surface of the warm curd. Let cool completely before adding it to the buttercream. The amount you use will depend on how lemony you want your buttercream.

> *TIP: Lemon curd used alone is not recommended for a wedding cake. Even with a dam it is risky to use it as a filling because it is too runny. It's good to mix it with buttercream.*

White-Chocolate Buttercream with Fresh Raspberries

• • •

Ingredients
One recipe for Italian Meringue

Melted white chocolate to taste, starting with an 8-ounce bar for 1 pound of butter

Method
If the white chocolate is in bar form, chop into pieces. White-chocolate chips are a little easier, so I do recommend those if possible. Put your chocolate in a double boiler, and stir gently over simmering water.

You can also use a metal bowl over a pot of simmering water. Stir the chocolate gently with a wire whisk or fork until melted and smooth.

> *TIP: Stir in a very small amount of vegetable oil to your white chocolate after melting to make it smoother.*

Raspberry Buttercream
Raspberry buttercream goes very well with the best chocolate-buttermilk cake and the best white-cake recipe.

To make raspberry buttercream, use a high-quality raspberry preserve, and mix it into your buttercream to taste, or add fresh or individually frozen raspberries to the layers as you fill them. It's easy and very delicious.

TIP: Raspberries are expensive. To stretch them out a bit, break them in half and then place them into the buttercream. Individually frozen raspberries work very well for this filling. You can cut them in half too.

Chocolate Buttercream

• • •

TO MAKE THE BEST CHOCOLATE buttercream, use the chocolate ganache recipe, and add it to your buttercream while it is still in the soft stage. If it has been refrigerated, place it in the microwave for a few minutes, stir and add it to the buttercream.

TIP: Use cocoa to make a light-chocolate buttercream or melted semisweet, bittersweet chocolate and/or a combination of the two.

AFTERWORD

• • •

I hope this book has helped to simplify the wedding-cake construction process for you. I gave you the basics with minimal cake-decorating techniques, assuming that you have never made a wedding cake before. With this information, you can create a beautiful and delicious cake. The recipes are tried and true and get rave reviews every time. Visit weddingcakesforyou.com for more information on baking and decorating and to join my newsletter or private cake-support group.

If you enjoyed this book and found it helpful, please take a moment to let me know. Please leave a review or send me an e-mail through my contact page anytime.

ABOUT THE AUTHOR

• • •

Lorelie Carvey is the creator and author of the website wedding-cakes-for-you.com. Carvey teaches cake decorating, baking, and also creates delicious cake and pastry recipes.

In 1985 Carvey first fell in love with cakes as chef at a French bakery in California and currently works out of her hometown in Connecticut. She is a Connecticut Chef's Association award-winning cake decorator and author of *Lorelie's Best Recipes in Extreme Detail*.

Made in the USA
Las Vegas, NV
25 September 2021